Contents

Emmeline Pankhurst 4

Childhood 6

Women 8

Family 10

The WSPU 12

Suffragette protests 14

In prison 16

Votes for women 18

Women's rights today 20

Quiz 22

Glossary 23

Index, answers and teaching notes . . . 24

Emmeline Pankhurst

Emmeline Pankhurst was a British **activist**. She organised **protests** to make life fairer for women.

Have you ever been to or seen a protest before? What was the protest about?

Before the early twentieth **century**, women in Great Britain could not **vote** in **elections**. Emmeline Pankhurst helped to change the **law** so that women could vote, just like men.

Suffragettes were women who fought for the right to vote. ▶

Childhood

Emmeline was born on 14 July 1858 in Manchester, England. She had nine brothers and sisters.

◀ Emmeline loved reading as a child.

How many children are there in your family?

Emmeline's family were interested in **politics**. When Emmeline was 14 years old, she went with her mother to a meeting about votes for women. The meeting **inspired** her to start fighting for women's rights.

▼ Many women went to meetings about votes for women at the time.

Women

When Emmeline was a young woman, women and men were treated differently. Most women didn't get a good education. Some people thought that women weren't as clever as men.

▼ Rich women, like Emmeline, were expected to stay at home and look after their families.

▲ Poorer women worked as cooks or cleaners, as well as looking after their families.

Married women also couldn't own their own **property**, such as houses or expensive objects.

▲ When a woman got married, everything she owned was given to her husband.

Family

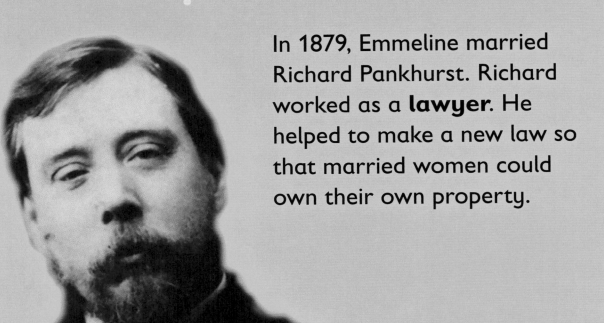

In 1879, Emmeline married Richard Pankhurst. Richard worked as a **lawyer**. He helped to make a new law so that married women could own their own property.

◀ Richard also fought for women's right to vote.

Adela

Sylvia

Christabel

Emmeline and Richard had five children — Christabel, Sylvia, Francis, Adela and Henry. Sadly, Francis died when he was four years old and Henry died at the age of 20.

◀ All three of Emmeline's daughters grew up to become suffragettes.

The WSPU

In 1903, Emmeline started a group called the WSPU (Women's Social and Political Union). The members of WSPU worked together to tell other people about women's rights.

▼ Emmeline's daughters Christabel and Sylvia helped her to run the WSPU.

Christabel

Sylvia

The WSPU believed that it wasn't enough to talk about wanting votes for women. They had to protest to show people that women's rights were important.

▼ **Suffragettes planned their protests in the WSPU offices.**

Do you belong to any groups or clubs?

Suffragette protests

The WSPU organised protests across Great Britain. They went on **marches** through towns and cities.

◀ Emmeline and other suffragettes gave speeches about women's rights.

The suffragettes carried banners saying 'Votes for Women'. ▶

People didn't listen, so the suffragettes decided to start doing protests that were more **disruptive**. They wanted people to pay attention to what they were saying.

▲ The suffragettes broke windows as a protest.

In prison

Emmeline

The suffragettes were often **arrested** for their disruptive protests. They were sent to prison.

◀ The suffragettes didn't want to stop their protests. The police had to carry them away.

Do you think it was right for the suffragettes to do disruptive protests?

It was hard for the suffragettes in prison. The **prison guards** didn't treat them well. But the suffragettes were prepared to go to prison if it made people listen to what they were saying.

Emmeline and her daughter Christabel were sent to prison several times. They had to wear a prison uniform. ▶

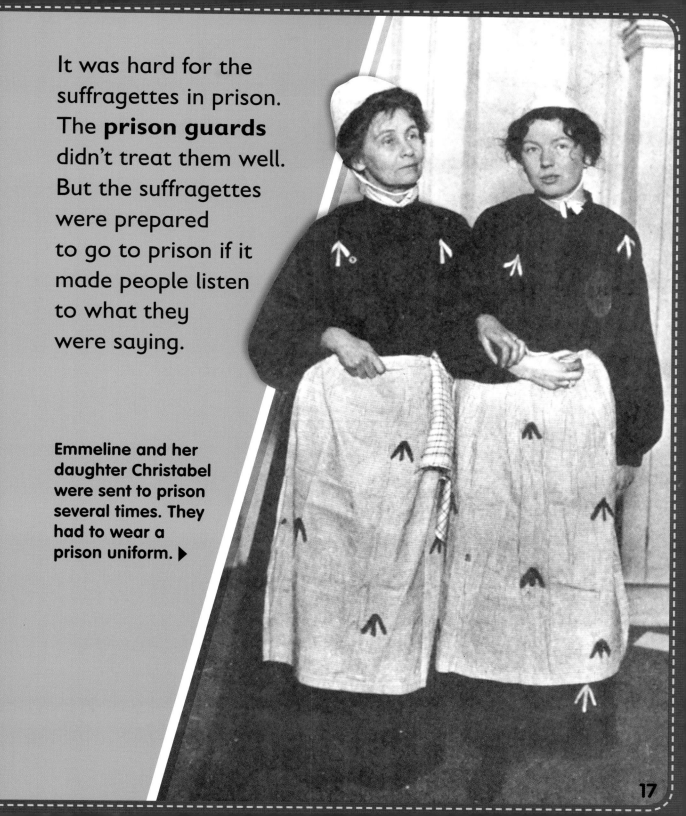

Votes for women

In 1914, the First World War started. Many suffragettes stopped protesting, as they were busy helping with the war. After the war ended in 1918, women over the age of 30 were given the right to vote.

◀ In 1918, women still didn't have the same rights as men. Men could vote at the age of 21.

Women helped a lot with the First World War. This helped to convince the government that they should be able to vote. ▶

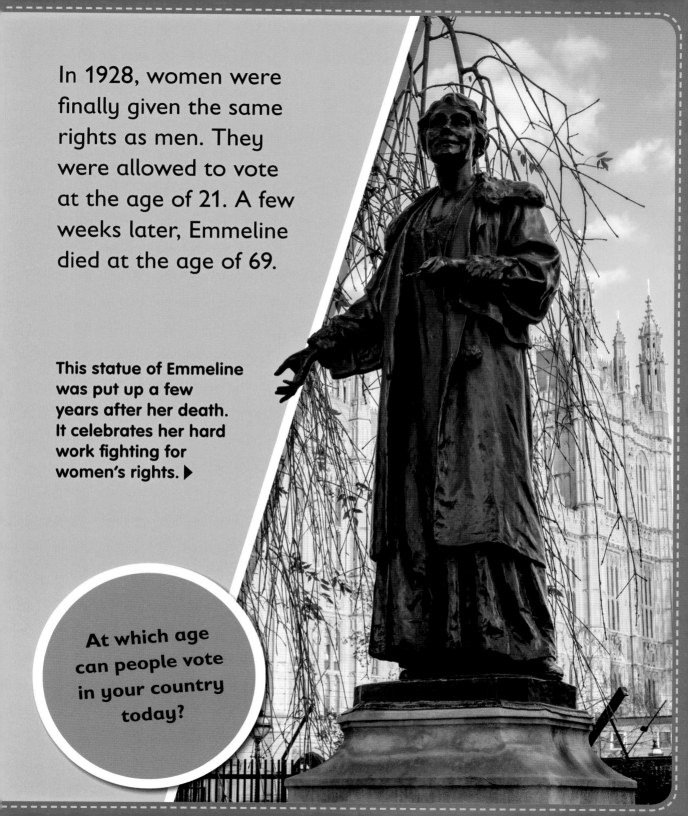

In 1928, women were finally given the same rights as men. They were allowed to vote at the age of 21. A few weeks later, Emmeline died at the age of 69.

This statue of Emmeline was put up a few years after her death. It celebrates her hard work fighting for women's rights. ▶

At which age can people vote in your country today?

Women's rights today

Thanks to people such as Emmeline Pankhurst, women and men have the same rights in most countries today. They can vote and own their own property.

Today, women are the leaders of some countries. Jacinda Ardern is the **prime minister** of New Zealand. ▶

However, life for some women is still difficult. Many women are not paid as much as men for doing the same job. In some countries, girls find it hard to get an education.

▲ People continue to protest to make women's lives better.

Quiz

Test how much you remember.

Check your answers on page 24.

1 How old was Emmeline when she went to her first women's rights meeting?

2 What were the names of Emmeline and Richard's children?

3 What does WSPU stand for?

4 Why were the suffragettes prepared to go to prison?

5 When did women over the age of 30 get the right to vote?

6 How old was Emmeline when she died?

Glossary

activist – someone who tries to change society

arrested – to be taken to a police station because the police think you have committed a crime

century – a period of one hundred years – the 20th century lasted from 1900 to 1999

disruptive – describes something that causes trouble and stops things from continuing as normal

election – the time when people vote to choose the leader of their country

inspire – to make someone else want to do something

law – a rule in a country

lawyer – someone whose job it is to understand the law

march – an organised walk by a group to show that they don't agree with something

politics – ideas about how a country is run by a government

prime minister – the leader of a country's government

prison guard – someone who looks after the prisoners in a prison

property – an object or objects that belong to someone

protest – doing something to show that you disagree with something

right – something that you can do or have according to the laws of your country

suffragette – a woman who protested for other women to be able to vote in elections

vote – to choose the person that you want to be in charge of your country

Index

arrest 16

childhood 6–7

education 8, 21

First World War 18

marches 14
marriage 9, 10
meetings 7

Pankhurst, Adela 11
Pankhurst, Christabel 11, 12, 17
Pankhurst, Richard 10, 11
Pankhurst, Sylvia 11, 12
prison 16, 17
protests 4, 13, 14–15, 16, 18, 21

rights 5, 7, 10, 12, 13, 14, 18, 19, 20

speeches 14
statue 19
suffragettes 5, 11, 13, 14, 15, 16, 17, 18

voting 5, 7, 10, 13, 14, 18–19, 20

WSPU, the 12, 13, 14

Answers:

1: 14 years old; 2: Christabel, Sylvia, Francis, Adela and Henry; 3: Women's Social and Political Union;
4: Because they thought going to prison would make people listen to what they were saying; 5: 1918;
6: 69 years old

Teaching notes:

Children who are reading Book Band Gold or above should be able to enjoy this book with some independence. Other children will need more support.

Before you share the book:

- Do children know what 'rights' are? Establish that 'rights' are something that everybody should have.

- Do they think that everyone should have the same rights, or should some people have more rights than others?

While you share the book:

- Help children to read some of the more unfamiliar words.

- Encourage children to think about how the rights the suffragettes fought for are useful.

- Talk about the different ways in which the suffragettes protested.

- Talk about the pictures. Discuss the differences between pictures from one hundred years ago and modern pictures.

After you have shared the book:

- Let children think about 'fairness'. Is it fair if some people have rights that other people don't have?

- Talk about the UN charter which gives rights to all children around the world, including the right to health, education, family life, play and recreation, an adequate standard of living, and to be protected from abuse and harm.

- Work through the free activity sheets at www.hachetteschools.co.uk

Franklin Watts
First published in Great Britain in 2020 by The Watts Publishing Group
Copyright © The Watts Publishing Group, 2020

Produced for Franklin Watts by
White-Thomson Publishing Ltd
www.wtpub.co.uk

ISBN: 978 1 4451 7209 5 (HB)
      978 1 4451 7272 9 (PB)

Credits
Series Editor: Izzi Howell
Series Designer: Rocket Design (East Anglia) Ltd
Designer: Clare Nicholas
Literacy Consultant: Kate Ruttle

The publisher would like to thank the following for permission to reproduce their pictures: Alamy: Trinity Mirror/Mirrorpix cover, Granger Historical Picture Archive 4, History collection 2016 6 and 10, Chronicle 11, Pictorial Press Ltd 12 and 14t; Getty: Photos.com title page, 14b, 16, 17 and 22, Hulton Archive/Stringer 5, duncan1890 7, whitemay 8l and 8r, TonyBaggett 9, Heritage Images 13, Photo 12 15; Shutterstock: Everett Historical 18t and 18b, Philip Bird LRPS CPAGB 19, photocosmos1 20, Ms Jane Campbell 21.

Every attempt has been made to clear copyright. Should there be any inadvertent omission please apply to the publisher for rectification.

Printed in Dubai

Franklin Watts
An imprint of
Hachette Children's Group
Part of The Watts Publishing Group
Carmelite House
50 Victoria Embankment
London EC4Y 0DZ

An Hachette UK Company
www.hachette.co.uk
www.franklinwatts.co.uk

All words in **bold** appear in the glossary on page 23.

Emmeline Pankhurst

Izzi Howell

W